Artists' Workshop

Crabtree Publishing Company

350 Fifth Avenue	360 York Road, R.R.4	73 Lime Walk
Suite 3308	Niagara-on-the-Lake	Headington, Oxford
New York, NY 10118	Ontario L0S 1J0	England OX3 7AD

Edited by **Bobbie Kalman**
Assistant Editor **Virginia Mainprize**
Designed by **Mei Lim**
Illustrations by **Lindy Norton**

Children's pictures by
**Emily Ashworth, Amy Browne, Vanessa Butselaar, Henrietta Chilton, Amber Civardi,
Charlotte Downham, Purdy Fitzherbert, Tamara Fitzherbert, Claudia Garrod, James Jarman,
Sophie Lewis, Alice Masson Taylor, Georgie Mew, Victoria Moss, Sam Pepper, Flora Pethybridge,
Susie Roberts, Camilla Schick, Georgina Smith, Thomas Stofer**

Picture research by **Sara Elliott**
Photographs by **Steve Shott**

Created by

Anne Civardi
Copyright © 1997 Anne Civardi

Cataloging-in-Publication Data

King, Penny, 1963-
Myths and legends/Penny King and Clare Roundhill
p. cm. – (Artists' Workshop)
Includes index.
Summary: Briefly retells six myths and legends from around the world
and presents art activities inspired by them.
ISBN 0-86505-865-2 (paper). – ISBN 0-86505-855-5 (RHB)
1. Legends in art – Juvenile literature. 2. Children's art-
– Juvenile literature.[1. Legends in art. 2. Art-Technique.]
I. Roundhill, Clare, 1964-   . II. Title. III Series: King, Penny. 1963- Artists' workshops.
N352.K53 1997   704.9'47-DC21   97-24691
CIP
AC

First published 1997 by
A & C Black (Publishers) Limited
35 Bedford Row, London WC1R 4JH

Printed in Hong Kong by Wing King Tong Co. Ltd

Cover photograph: **Antonio del Pollaiuolo** Apollo and Daphne c.1470- 1480
Antonio del Pollaiuolo and his brother, Piero, worked together for much of their lives. They ran a very
famous workshop in Florence, Italy, where other artists would come to learn new skills. Antonio was well-known for
his interest in drawing the human body. He was fascinated by the way muscles worked when people
moved and tried to show this in his paintings and sculptures.

Contents

The meaning of myths and legends

In this book, there are six exciting stories from around the world. Some are myths, others are legends.

The word 'myth' comes from the Greek word *muthos*, which means story.

Myths tell the story of imaginary people. Sometimes, they answer difficult and important questions, such as 'How did the world begin?' and 'From where did people first come?'

Legends are stories about events in real people's lives. Even when these people were still alive, stories were told of their brave deeds.

Over the years, as different people told these tales, they added details to make them sound more exciting. They left out the dull parts. Soon fact became confused with fiction.

Many myths and legends from different parts of the world sound the same. There are many stories of heroes setting out on exciting journeys that last many years. Stories about a god punishing a sinful world by sending a great flood are found in the Bible as well as in Chinese myths. The more myths and legends you read, the more you will discover how alike many are.

The six myths and legends in this book each tell a wonderful story. You will find out how a little bird helped create the world. You will read the myth of a girl who was chased by an unwanted admirer. You will share the adventures of Sinbad who faced terrible dangers on his voyages across the sea. And you will meet a hero who saved the world.

You will see what happened to Alexander when he was lowered into the sea in a glass barrel. You will learn about King Arthur and his Knights of the Round Table.

Six artists have used different techniques to illustrate these stories. After reading the stories and looking at the illustrations, use their ideas and yours to create your own art.

Underwater escape

Imagine all the wonderful creatures you would see if you were in a glass barrel deep under the ocean! This picture comes from a very old book of legends. It tells the adventures of Alexander the Great.

The Legendary Journeys of Alexander the Great from The Old French Prose Alexander Romance 1445. By permission of The British Library, London

During the Middle Ages, books were very expensive. The words as well as the pictures in a book were painted by hand. Skilled artists used paints made from natural materials, such as coal, chalk, pure gold and precious stones.

In those days, most people could not read. They heard tales from storytellers. Large crowds would gather in the town square to listen to traveling minstrels tell their tales. Sometimes, these stories were performed as plays.

Alexander the Great

Alexander the Great was born in 356 BC, in Macedonia, which is now part of Greece. Although he was only 32 years old when he died, Alexander is still a well-known hero. He was a brave and famous soldier. He led his troops into many battles and conquered half of Asia. During his life, people told stories of Alexander's victories in battle. In the centuries that followed, these tales became more legend than truth.

One tale tells of Alexander walking along the seashore. He found an enormous crab holding some fabulous pearls in its claws. Dreaming of more riches from the sea, Alexander made himself a large glass barrel. Crouched inside the barrel, Alexander was lowered by a long chain from his ship to the bottom of the sea. As soon as he had found some jewels, he planned to push his hand through a small hole in the barrel, grab the treasure, plug up the hole and return to his ship.

Suddenly, an enormous fish, with a mouth as big as a whale's, swam up to the barrel. To Alexander's horror, the fish clamped the glass barrel in its gigantic jaws and swam away, dragging the ship along. On reaching the shore, the mighty fish crushed the barrel with its sharp teeth and spat it onto the land. Although he was terribly shaken, Alexander was safe. He vowed to be much more careful in future.

Secrets of the sea

Create your own underwater pictures to go with the legend of Alexander inside his glass barrel. Think about the strange colors, patterns and shapes of all the fish, corals and plants he might have seen deep in the sea.

The deep, blue sea

Use wax crayons to draw Alexander in his glass barrel in the sea. Show his ship floating above him. Color in everything except the sky and the sea. Press hard to make the colors really bright. Cover the sky with blue paint. Make the paint lighter by adding a little water and fill in the sea.

Life in the sea

Sketch an underwater scene. Imagine strangely shaped plants, twisting corals, weird sea creatures, beautiful fish and a gleaming palace.

Use your sketch to create a bright and colorful picture. Make the plants and corals from torn tissue paper and the sea creatures and fish from shiny candy wrappers. Paint the palace and decorate it with golden glitter.

Tissue paper fish

Draw the shape of a huge fish on colored paper. Tear lots of fish-scale shapes from brightly colored tissue paper. Glue them on the fish in overlapping rows. Add sequin eyes and frilly fins made from more torn tissue.

9

Love lessons

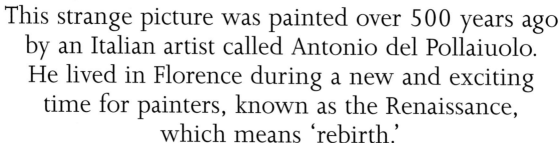

This strange picture was painted over 500 years ago by an Italian artist called Antonio del Pollaiuolo. He lived in Florence during a new and exciting time for painters, known as the Renaissance, which means 'rebirth.'

Antonio del Pollaiuolo Apollo and Daphne c.1470-1480. Reproduced by courtesy of the Trustees, The National Gallery, London

Many Renaissance artists painted stories from ancient Roman and Greek myths. This painting tells the story of Apollo, the Greek god of the sun, and Daphne, a beautiful river nymph. Notice how the artist used light and shade to make the picture look real.

Pollaiuolo was also a fine jewelry-maker, sculptor and drawer. Like many other Renaissance artists, he had a large workshop where he trained young apprentices. Artists from Florence often visited each others' workshops to share their skills and ideas.

Apollo and Daphne

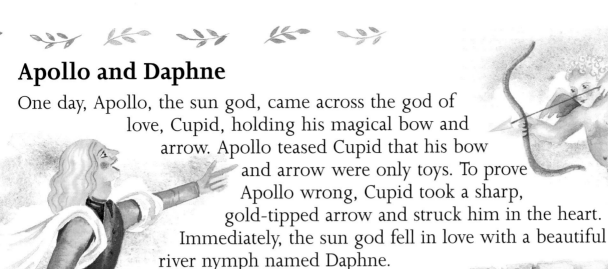

One day, Apollo, the sun god, came across the god of love, Cupid, holding his magical bow and arrow. Apollo teased Cupid that his bow and arrow were only toys. To prove Apollo wrong, Cupid took a sharp, gold-tipped arrow and struck him in the heart. Immediately, the sun god fell in love with a beautiful river nymph named Daphne.

To make sure that Daphne would never fall in love with Apollo, Cupid drew his bow once more and pierced her heart with a blunt, lead-tipped arrow. Apollo begged Daphne to be his love, but the nymph ran away from him, deep into the forest. The faster she raced, the more Apollo fell in love with her.

Daphne ran and ran, her eyes shining brightly and her hair falling around her shoulders like golden clouds. Apollo ran after her, following close behind. Soon Daphne began to tire. Not able to bear the thought of giving up her freedom, she called to her father, the river god. She begged him to save her. Instantly, her arms began to stiffen and her feet started to twist and root themselves in the earth.

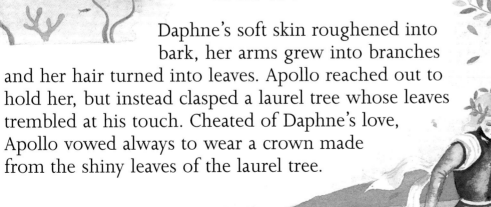

Daphne's soft skin roughened into bark, her arms grew into branches and her hair turned into leaves. Apollo reached out to hold her, but instead clasped a laurel tree whose leaves trembled at his touch. Cheated of Daphne's love, Apollo vowed always to wear a crown made from the shiny leaves of the laurel tree.

The art of love

Make a cupid card to send to someone special on Valentine's Day. Choose your favorite part of the myth of Apollo and Daphne and create your own pictures of a river god, a sun god or of Daphne turning into a laurel tree.

Valentine card

Make a card out of red, pink or gold paper. Decorate it with bits and pieces, such as ribbon, lacy paper, fake fur fabric, feathers, paper shapes and sequins. Draw a cupid on black paper and cut it out. Make a bow and arrow out of twisted silver foil and stick them and the cupid onto the card. Add a special message to your Valentine card. Send it in an envelope decorated with tissue-paper hearts.

River god

On blue paper, draw an outline of a river god with a fish tail. Cover the top half of his body with glue and sprinkle on glitter. Create a strange-looking face from wrapping paper and sequins. Make the god's bushy hair from Christmas tinsel. Cover his fish tail with colored paper scales. Add sequin eyes.

Cut fish shapes out of a flat sponge and use them to print brightly colored fish all over the background.

Leafy Daphne

Divide a white sheet of paper into three sections. In the first, draw a picture of Daphne in her beautiful robes with her long, flowing hair. In the second, show her arms beginning to stiffen and her feet starting to twist. In the third, show Daphne turned into a laurel tree with rough branches for arms and green, leafy hair.

Divine dragon

This wiggling dragon is made from ceramic tiles. It was created to decorate part of the Nine Dragon Wall in the Forbidden City in Beijing, China. It shows part of a story about a hero called Yu the Great who was half-dragon and half-human.

Nine Dragon Wall Forbidden City Beijing, China. 15th Century

According to myth, Yu the Great defeated the evil Spirit of the Waters. Because he saved the world from a terrible flood, Yu was made Emperor of China. In Chinese art the Emperor is often shown as a dragon.

The Emperor of China was very powerful. He lived in a magnificent palace surrounded by three sets of thick walls within the Forbidden City. Only the Emperor and his servants could enter this special place.

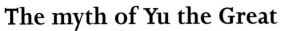

The myth of Yu the Great

The Yellow Emperor, who ruled heaven, was angry with the wickedness of people. He decided to send a terrible flood to destroy the world.

Only Kun, the Emperor's grandson, took pity on the people. He begged his grandfather to stop the rain, but the Emperor would not listen. So Kun stole some of his grandfather's magic earth and threw it into the floodwaters. Immediately, land began to appear, soaking up the water.

When the Emperor discovered what Kun had done, he had him killed and sent an even worse flood to earth. Day after day, lightning streaked across the sky. Booming thunder echoed through the mountains, and huge waves of water crashed against the mountainsides. The people picked up their soaked possessions and carried them to the top of the highest mountain.

Far away, out of Kun's dead body, leapt his son, a mighty dragon called Yu. Yu soared up to heaven and persuaded his great-grandfather to stop the flood. When Yu returned to earth as a human, however, he found even more water. Gigantic waves crashed over the mountaintops, and many people had drowned in the flood. It was the work of an evil demon called the Spirit of the Waters who wanted to destroy the world. But Yu, helped by an army of spirits, defeated him just in time.

Yu built rivers and dams, lakes and streams to carry the floodwaters away. The mountains, hills and fields were dry again. Now the people had somewhere to live and land to farm. The world was safe.

Heroes and floods

Use the beautiful colors and shapes of the dragon in the Nine Dragon Wall picture to create your own One Dragon Wall out of self-hardening clay.

You could also make a dragon from bits and pieces you find around the house. Or you can create a flooded landscape picture by using a comb to drag thick paint across cardboard.

Dragon tiles
Fold a large square of paper into four squares and then unfold it. Over all four squares, draw a simple sketch of a wiggling dragon with bulging eyes, scales and a tongue.

Roll out a large ball of self-hardening clay into a flat square about ¼ inch thick (8 mm). Use more clay to make the body of the dragon. Add eyes, tongue and scales. Look at your sketch to help you. Press the shapes onto the clay square. You may need to wet the clay to make the shapes stick. While the clay is still wet, cut it into four equal squares. Leave the clay to harden. Paint the dragon bright colors.

Dragon sculpture

Create a wiggling dragon sculpture by taping together small cereal boxes, cardboard rolls and little yogurt cartons. Cover them with silver foil. Then decorate the dragon's body with feathers, sequins, braid and tinsel. You can also use pieces of tissue and wrapping paper.

Flooded landscape

Mix flour and liquid glue with paint to make it really thick. Cut out cardboard combs with different shaped teeth, as shown.

With a fat brush, paint green hills, dark blue rivers and a bright blue sky on white paper. While the paint is wet, use the combs to scratch patterns in the hills, like those on the Nine Dragon Wall tiles. Make wavy patterns in the rivers and cloudy patterns in the sky.

17

Sacred shields

This decorated shield is a copy of one made long ago by the Cheyenne Indians of North America. The picture shows the story of the creation of the earth by the Great Spirit, whom the Cheyennes believed to be the maker of the universe.

Cheyenne The Earth Diver c. 19th century. The Field Museum, Chicago

Cheyenne Indians led lives filled with danger and needed protection from their enemies and wild animals. A shield, made from buffalo hide, was a brave's most valued possession. He believed it had great spiritual powers.

Shields decorated with pictures of eagles and real eagle feathers were believed to give their owner the power, grace and speed of an eagle. Those painted with bears were thought to give strength and courage.

The myth of the Great Spirit

In the beginning, the Great Spirit created the Great Water. There was no sun, no moon and no day, just darkness and the cold, salty sea. Only sea creatures and birds existed. Soon, the birds grew tired of flying in the air and went in search of land. The only place where land could possibly be was deep down in the icy water. Again and again, powerful eagles, owls and vultures dived into the dark sea. Each time they failed to find land.

Finally, a little coot arrived. Taking a mighty breath, he dived into the dark waters. Down and down the coot went, until he spotted a huge lump of earth. Almost out of breath, the bird snatched a tiny speck and returned to the top.

As he burst through the icy water, the coot saw the Great Spirit glimmering in the darkness. Taking the speck of earth from the bird, the Spirit began to roll it in his hands. The speck began to grow, first into a boulder, then into a mountain, and finally into the whole world. Too heavy for the Spirit to carry, he rested it on Grandmother Turtle's back. Her powerful legs carried its huge weight. The world was safe.

Then, the Great Spirit filled the world with animals, insects and reptiles of all kinds. Lush forests began to grow, full of colorful birds, fruits and flowers. Finally, into the sky the Great Spirit tossed a burning sun. Under its warm glow, the world started its first day.

Cheyenne creations

Imagine that you need a shield to give you special powers or good luck. You could draw a turtle or eagle on your shield and decorate it with feathers, bells, beads and ribbons. You could also create a picture of what you think the Great Spirit looked like.

Magic shield

Draw a turtle or eagle in the middle of a large white cardboard circle. Decorate it with paper shapes. Use felt-tipped pens to draw waves of power from the creature's feet. Color the background with wax crayons, leaving white spaces around the creature and the power lines. Hang feathers, bells, beads, sequins and scraps of fabric onto the shield on pieces of colored wool. Add a loop of ribbon to the top. Hang your shield on your bedroom door.

A storm of birds

Fold a sheet of blue paper in half lengthwise. Open it up again. On one half, use thick paint and a wide brush to create shapes of birds swooping down to the sea. Before the paint dries, fold the paper again and press the two halves together. Open up the paper and let the paint dry. Use a fine brush to paint in the birds' beaks, feet and eyes.

The Great Spirit

On colored paper, draw the outline of the shape you think the Great Spirit might be. To make your picture really shimmer, decorate it with tissue-paper circles, sequins, glitter, shiny paper and tassels.

Kings and knights

This richly colored stained-glass panel was designed by Edward Burne-Jones and made by William Morris. Both men were 19th-century, English artists. They created the glass panel in the same way as the windows of churches were made hundreds of years before.

Edward Burne-Jones and William Morris *Arthurian Legends* c. 1880–1890. By courtesy of the Board of Trustees of the Victoria and Albert Museum, London

The panel shows a story from the legend of King Arthur. In the picture, Sir Lancelot, one of the Knights of the Round Table, is with the king's wife, Queen Guinevere. Although he was Arthur's most trusted knight, Lancelot was deeply in love with Guinevere.

The angel in the red robe is holding a magical golden goblet called the Holy Grail. All the Knights of the Round Table wanted to find this priceless treasure. They believed it would heal their battle wounds and help them live forever.

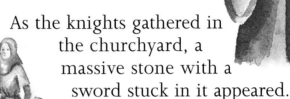

The adventures of King Arthur

When Arthur was a tiny baby, his father, King Uther, told his friend Merlin, the wise magician, that he feared a plot to kill the child. He asked Merlin to hide Arthur. When Uther died, only Merlin knew that the king had a son to inherit his crown.

Throughout the land, knights began to fight each other for the right to become the new king. On hearing this, Merlin asked the Lord Archbishop of Britain to bring the knights to London.

As the knights gathered in the churchyard, a massive stone with a sword stuck in it appeared. Only the true king of England would be able to pull the sword out of the stone. Many of the strongest knights tried and could not remove the sword.

So the Archbishop decided to hold a tournament to find the next king. Arthur's brother decided to enter. On his way, Arthur's brother realized he had forgotten his sword. Arthur offered to go back and fetch it. As he passed the churchyard, the boy saw the gleaming sword in the stone. He ran up to it and pulled it out without any trouble. At last, the true King of England had been found.

One day, during battle, King Arthur's sword snapped in two. When Arthur told Merlin, the magician took him to a mysterious lake. As Arthur stared at the water, a hand appeared holding a magnificent jewelled sword. Then a beautiful woman, the Lady of the Lake, rose from the water. She walked across the lake and handed the sword to Arthur. The new sword was called Excalibur.

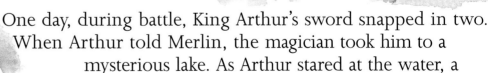

Stained-glass secrets

To make the stained-glass panel, William Morris cut thin sheets of colored glass. He attached them to each other using strips of lead — the dark lines you can see in the picture on page 22.

Use glowing colors to create your own pictures from the stories of King Arthur and his knights.

Glowing jewels

On black or gold construction paper, draw the outline of one of the objects in the story, such as the Holy Grail goblet, the jewelled sword or a crown. Cut it out. Draw jewel shapes on the back of the goblet, sword or crown. Carefully cut out the shapes with small scissors. Glue colored tissue-paper over the jewel-shaped holes on the back of the card. Hang your picture in a window where the light will shine through it.

Felt-tipped pen window

Choose a character from the story of King Arthur. Draw him or her on white paper. Place a sheet of thick tracing paper over it and keep the papers together with a paper clip. Trace the character's outline with a black felt-tipped pen. Color the rest of the picture. Frame your picture with black construction paper. Hang it in a window.

Stained-glass picture

Lightly sketch the outlines of a scene from the story of King Arthur. Use a pencil and white paper. On top of your picture mark out where the 'lead' of the stained-glass window might go. Look at the picture of Lancelot and Guinevere on page 22 to help you. Decorate each section with different colors and patterns using felt-tipped pens. Darken the 'lead' lines with a black felt-tipped pen.

Arabian adventures

The English artist Edward Detmold painted this scene
for a beautiful book called Arabian Nights.
The picture shows part of the story of a dangerous
voyage of Sinbad the Sailor.

E J Detmold The Voyages of Sinbad from The Arabian Nights. Tales from the Thousand and One Nights 1924. By permission of the British Library, London

Detmold had a twin brother who was
also a fine illustrator. From the age of
five, the boys made many trips to the
London zoo to study and sketch
animals. Their uncle, who was
fascinated by nature, encouraged the
boys to study plants as well as animals.

The painting is not only beautiful
but also looks very real. Notice the
care Detmold has taken to show the
rough bark of the trees and the
different shaped leaves. The brightly
colored turbans, parrots and flowers
stand out from the green of the jungle.

The adventures of Sinbad

Searching for adventure and riches, Sinbad sailed off on seven voyages around the world. He travelled for 27 years. He escaped death, survived many dangers, defeated vicious monsters and tricked evil villains.

On his first voyage, Sinbad and his crew landed on a beautiful island. There they lit a fire to cook a fine feast. Suddenly, the whole island began to shake and shudder. Too late, the sailors realized that it was not an island at all, but a huge, angry whale. Luckily, Sinbad escaped to another island. There he made friends with the king, Mahrajan, who gave him great riches.

Years later, stranded alone on another island, Sinbad came across a gleaming white palace. As he walked around it, he was surprised to find no windows or doors. All at once, the sky turned black and Sinbad was knocked to the ground by a mighty wind. Hovering above him was a Roc - a bird so huge that it fed elephants to its babies. Only when the Roc settled on the massive white object did Sinbad realize that it was not a palace, but the giant bird's egg.

On his last voyage, Sinbad was captured by an evil trader who forced him to hunt and kill elephants for their valuable ivory tusks. A wise old bull elephant, anxious to stop the killing, took Sinbad to the elephant graveyard, deep in the forest. Here, Sinbad saw piles of bones and curved tusks. When he told his master about this secret place, the trader was so delighted that he gave Sinbad his freedom, a rich reward and vowed never to kill another elephant.

Voyages in art

Create your own illustrations to go with the stories of Sinbad. Looking at pictures of wild animals in magazines and books may help you begin. Try to imagine some of the terrifying monsters Sinbad met on his voyages. Perhaps they had razor-sharp teeth, huge, curved claws and strange-looking bodies.

Fantastic forest

To create a jungle scene, draw the outline of one or two parrots on a piece of colored construction paper. Cut them out and glue them onto a piece of dark construction paper. Cut or tear out feathers from colored tissue-paper and glue them onto the parrot. Paint on a yellow beak and outline it with a black felt-tipped pen. Add some eyes. Cut out lots of green tissue-paper leaves. Glue them by the stem only around the parrot.

Sunset silhouette

Using shades of red and orange paint, brush wide streaks of each color onto a white background. Paint darker streaks at the top and lighter ones at the bottom. While the paint is drying, draw a big egg shape on white paper. Cut it out and glue it onto the background, as shown.

Use a white crayon to draw a huge Roc on black paper. Give it sharp claws and a curved beak. Cut out the bird and glue it above the white egg. Paint on a big bloodshot eye!

Elephant ride

Use a felt-tipped pen to draw an elephant's body or head on a piece of gray felt. Cut it out and glue it onto colored paper. On white paper, draw a picture of Sinbad to sit on the elephant. Decorate his clothes and turban with fabric scraps. Cut him out and glue him on top of the elephant. You may glue on felt or paper leaves and grass.

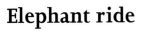

More about the artists and pictures

Alexander's Submarine
(1445)
The Talbot Master

The Talbot Master was the name given to the illustrator of the picture of Alexander in his glass barrel. He was the favorite artist of the English Earl of Shrewsbury, John Talbot. The Master worked in the town of Rouen, in France and painted 83 illustrations for the stories of Alexander. This book was given, probably as a wedding present, to Queen Margaret of Anjou on her marriage to Henri VI in 1445.

Apollo and Daphne
(Probably 1470-1480)
Antonio del Pollaiuolo   1432/3 - 1498

Pollaiuolo was an Italian painter, sculptor, engraver and goldsmith. He was famous for his lifelike pictures showing people in motion. Pollaiuolo drew his models stretching and bending so that he could see their muscles bulge beneath their skin. He even studied dead bodies, cutting them up to see how the bones and muscles joined together. This helped him make his pictures more real. Later, other artists did the same, but Pollaiuolo was among the first to be so scientific in his art.

Nine Dragon Wall
(15th Century)
Forbidden City, Beijing, China

The Nine Dragon Wall was a large and expensive project. Many people helped build it. First the court artist drew plans for the Emperor. When the Emperor approved them, they were sent to the province of Shanxi, which is famous for its tile making. A team of artists made the tiles out of clay, using special tools. The tiles were then painted with colored glazes and fired in a kiln.

The Earth Diver
Cheyenne Shield   19th century

A sacred shield could be made only by a trained shield-maker, working in a special lodge. The shield-maker sang sacred songs and smoked a special pipe as he built his shield. Before he displayed the finished shield for the tribe to see, he rubbed white clay all over his body and decorated himself with bird feathers. The shield was kept outside the owner's lodge. It was turned to face the sun.

Arthurian Legends
(1880-1890)
William Morris   1834-1896
Edward Burne-Jones   1833-1898

William Morris and Edward Burne-Jones met when they were students at Oxford University in England. They became life-long friends and shared a deep love of tales of chivalry, especially those about King Arthur and his Knights of the Round Table. Together they created many paintings and stained-glass pictures of these stories to decorate the walls and ceilings of churches.

Sinbad the Sailor
(1924)
Edward Julius Detmold   1883-1957

Edward and his twin brother, Charles, worked together on illustrations for storybooks until Charles died suddenly at the age of twenty-four. After his brother's death, Edward began experimenting with wood-block printing, engraving and still-life painting. However, he continued to illustrate children's books. He especially enjoyed painting animals and plants, like those in the Jungle Book, Arabian Nights and Aesop's Fables.

Other things to do

3 Create your own mythical monster by drawing a monster face on some colorful paper. Glue on scrunched-up silver foil eyes, foil teeth, shiny paper spots and wool hair. Color the face with felt-tipped pens.

1 To make a fine treasure chest, paint a small box and lid a bright color. Put a thick layer of glue all over the outside of the box and press sequins, paper shapes, beads and glitter into it. Make a fancy key from twisted silver foil and attach it to the box with ribbon. Now you have a place for your treasures.

2 Sketch a picture of how you think a mythical land might look. Draw all kinds of mythical creatures, strange-looking birds, odd trees and plants, as well as flowers and fruits. Color in your picture with brightly colored felt-tipped pens.

4 To make a creation globe, mix flour, water and glue into a thick paste. Dip newspaper strips into the paste and stick them onto a big blown-up balloon. Overlap six layers of strips, coating the last layer with paste. Let the paste dry.

Paint oceans, icebergs, deserts, forests, mountains and land on your globe. Cut out paper animals, color them and stick them all over the globe.